T0390108

# NEW ENGLAND PATRIOTS

MATT SCHEFF

Apex is distributed by North Star Editions:
sales@northstareditions.com | 888-417-0195

Produced for Apex by Red Line Editorial.

Photographs ©: Damian Strohmeyer/AP Images, cover, 1; Greg M. Cooper/AP Images, 4–5, 58–59; Kathryn Riley/Getty Images Sport/Getty Images, 6–7; Bettmann/Getty Images, 8–9; Richard Stagg/Getty Images Sport/Getty Images, 10–11; Focus On Sport/Getty Images Sport/Getty Images, 12–13, 20–21, 26–27, 32–33; Rob Brown/Getty Images Sport/Getty Images, 14–15; Winslow Townson/Panini/AP Images, 16–17, 37, 57; Ezra O. Shaw/Allsport/Getty Images Sport/Getty Images, 19; George Gojkovich/Getty Images Sport/Getty Images, 22–23; Bill Smith/Getty Images Sport/Getty Images, 24–25; Rick Bowmer/AP Images, 28–29; Elsa/Getty Images Sport/Getty Images, 30–31, 38–39, 40–41; Joe Sargent/Getty Images Sport/Getty Images, 34–35; Jared Wickerham/Getty Images Sport/Getty Images, 42–43, 47; Cooper Neill/Getty Images Sport/Getty Images, 44–45; Billie Weiss/Getty Images Sport/Getty Images, 48–49; Shutterstock Images, 50–51; Maddie Meyer/Getty Images Sport/Getty Images, 52–53; Mike Ehrmann/Getty Images Sport/Getty Images, 54–55

**Library of Congress Control Number: 2024939370**

**ISBN**
979-8-89250-155-2 (hardcover)
979-8-89250-172-9 (paperback)
979-8-89250-296-2 (ebook pdf)
979-8-89250-189-7 (hosted ebook)

Printed in the United States of America
Mankato, MN
012025

## NOTE TO PARENTS AND EDUCATORS

Apex books are designed to build literacy skills in striving readers. Exciting, high-interest content attracts and holds readers' attention. The text is carefully leveled to allow students to achieve success quickly.

# TABLE OF CONTENTS

# CHAPTER 1

# LET'S GO PATS!

The stands are filled with New England Patriots fans. It's a sea of red, white, and blue. A chant of "Let's go Pats!" fills the stadium. The fans cheer on their team as the clock ticks down.

**More than 65,000 fans can fit inside the Patriots' stadium.**

Patriots linebacker Matthew Judon sacks the quarterback in a 2022 game against the Lions.

New England's defense is on the field. The Patriots need a big stop. The crowd gets louder and louder. Soon, the ball is snapped. Defenders crash in on the quarterback. It's a sack! The fans go wild. The Patriots are one step closer to victory.

## WHY NEW ENGLAND?

The Patriots started out in the city of Boston, Massachusetts. So, the team was called the Boston Patriots. In 1971, the Pats moved to the nearby town of Foxborough. They changed their name to the New England Patriots. New England is a large region. It includes six states.

# CHAPTER 2

# EARLY HISTORY

The Boston Patriots started playing in 1960. They were part of the AFL. This league was separate from the NFL. The Patriots were one of the AFL's first eight teams.

The Patriots (dark jerseys) didn't have their own stadium in the 1960s. They played home games at different spots in the Boston area.

Tom Hennessey (30) returns an interception in a 1965 game against the San Diego Chargers.

The Patriots didn't have much success in the AFL. They made the playoffs only once. In 1963, they beat the Buffalo Bills to win the East Division. Then they went to the AFL title game. But the San Diego Chargers won easily.

## CHOOSING A NAME

The team let fans help choose a name. Many people sent in ideas. The team decided on the Patriots. The name honored those who fought in the American Revolutionary War (1775–1783).

The AFL and NFL joined together in 1970. The next year, the Boston Patriots changed their name to the New England Patriots. The team continued to struggle, though. In 1984, the Patriots decided it was time for a new head coach. They hired Raymond Berry.

## COACH CAN CATCH

Raymond Berry was an excellent receiver for the Baltimore Colts in the 1950s and 1960s. After he stopped playing, Berry spent many years as a wide receivers coach. He got his first head coaching job with the Patriots.

Tony Eason (11) threw for 3,228 yards and 23 touchdowns in 1984.

Berry led the Patriots to the playoffs in 1985. In the first round, they beat the New York Jets. Next, they defeated the Los Angeles Raiders. Then they beat the Miami Dolphins to reach the Super Bowl. But the magical season ended in disappointment. The Patriots fell to the Chicago Bears 46–10.

## ROAD WARRIORS

The Patriots didn't win their division in 1985. But they made the playoffs as a wild card. All three of their playoff games were on the road. And the Patriots won all three games. No team in NFL history had done that before.

The Patriots forced six turnovers in their playoff game against the Raiders.

Head coach Bill Parcells joined the Patriots in 1993. So did rookie quarterback Drew Bledsoe. In 1996, they led New England to an 11–5 record. The Patriots made it all the way to the Super Bowl that season. But the Green Bay Packers were too strong. They beat New England 35–21. Parcells left the team after that season.

**Patriots players soak Bill Parcells after winning the conference title game in the 1996 season.**

# DREW BLEDSOE

The Patriots had the first pick in the 1993 draft. They chose Drew Bledsoe. The quarterback was known for his strong arm. He also had great accuracy. Bledsoe quickly became one of the league's best passers.

Bledsoe helped New England reach the playoffs four times in his first six years. His best season came in 1994. He led the NFL in passing yards. He also led in completions.

Bledsoe spent nine seasons with New England. During that time, he made the Pro Bowl three times.

**DREW BLEDSOE TOPPED 29,000 PASSING YARDS DURING HIS TIME WITH THE PATRIOTS.**

# CHAPTER 3

# LEGENDS

**G**ino Cappelletti was the Patriots' first real star. Cappelletti played wide receiver. He was also the team's kicker. His finest season came in 1964. He scored seven touchdowns that year. He also booted 25 field goals.

Gino Cappelletti led the league in made field goals in three different seasons.

Guard John Hannah was one of the top linemen of his era. He made the Pro Bowl nine times between 1976 and 1985. Mike Haynes was a star defensive back and punt returner. He grabbed 28 interceptions in seven seasons with New England.

## SIZE DOESN'T MATTER

No one expected much from linebacker Nick Buoniconti. Many thought he was too small to play pro football. But he thrived with the Patriots. Buoniconti had quickness and good hands. Those skills helped him collect 24 interceptions for New England.

In 13 seasons, John Hannah (73) missed only five games due to injuries.

Linebacker Andre Tippett was the heart of New England's defense in the 1980s. Tippett recorded 100 sacks. That's a team record.

Quarterback Tony Eason led the Patriots to their first Super Bowl. Stanley Morgan was one of his favorite targets. The receiver averaged 19.4 yards per catch as a Patriot.

## SAVING THE PATRIOTS

In the early 1990s, owner James Orthwein planned to move the Patriots. The team would have become the St. Louis Stallions. However, Robert Kraft blocked the move. Kraft was the owner of the Patriots' stadium. In 1994, Kraft bought the team.

In 1979, Stanley Morgan led the NFL with 12 touchdown catches.

25

**Curtis Martin won the Offensive Rookie of the Year Award in 1995.**

Quarterback Drew Bledsoe led a strong offense in the 1990s. Terry Glenn was one of his top targets. Glenn was a speedy receiver. He could blow past defenses. Running back Curtis Martin was a dual-threat back. Martin was a tough runner. He was also a good pass catcher.

## UNIFORM CHANGE

The Patriots' original colors were red, white, and blue. They honored the American flag. In 1993, the Patriots made some changes. They added silver pants to their uniforms. They also changed from red to blue home jerseys.

# CHAPTER 4

# RECENT HISTORY

In 2000, the Patriots hired head coach Bill Belichick. A year later, Tom Brady took over for the injured Drew Bledsoe. The Patriots went on a surprising run to the Super Bowl. A strong defense helped them shock the powerful St. Louis Rams. It was New England's first Super Bowl title.

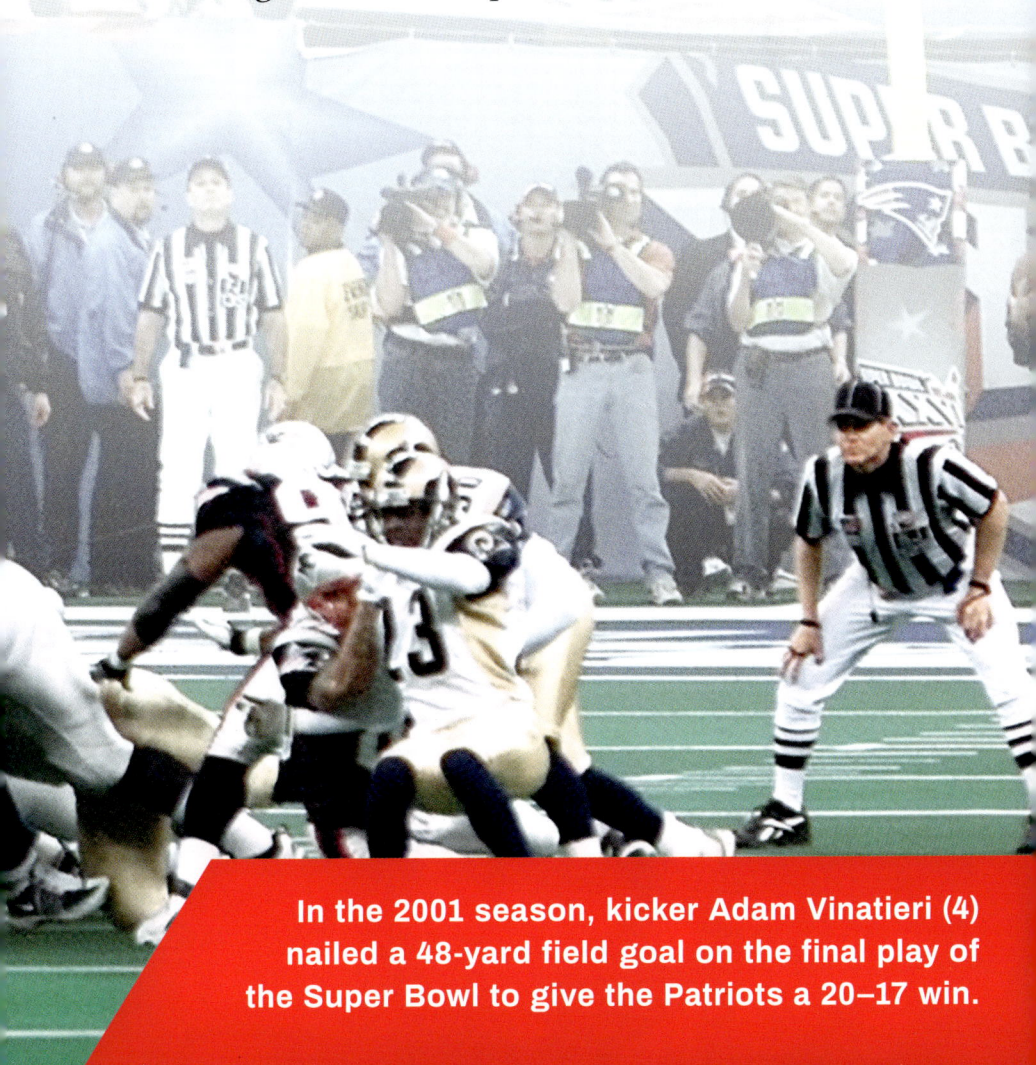

In the 2001 season, kicker Adam Vinatieri (4) nailed a 48-yard field goal on the final play of the Super Bowl to give the Patriots a 20–17 win.

Tom Brady (12) threw three touchdown passes in New England's Super Bowl win over the Panthers.

New England built a dynasty. In the 2003 season, the Patriots returned to the Super Bowl. They beat the Carolina Panthers to win their second title. The Patriots made it back to the big game the next year. This time, they beat the Philadelphia Eagles.

## ALMOST PERFECT

The 2007 Patriots seemed unstoppable. Brady and receiver Randy Moss put up amazing numbers. The team went 16–0 in the regular season. But their chance at a perfect season ended in the Super Bowl. The New York Giants scored a touchdown in the game's final minute. They stunned New England 17–14.

In the 2014 season, Malcolm Butler (21) intercepted a pass with 20 seconds left, sealing a Super Bowl win over the Seahawks.

The Patriots' success continued in the 2010s. From 2009 to 2019, the team won 11 straight division titles. During that time, the Patriots went to the Super Bowl five times. They won three of them. It was one of the greatest dynasties in football history.

## HUGE RIVALRY

The Patriots and the Indianapolis Colts had a huge rivalry in the 2000s. They also had two of the best quarterbacks in NFL history. Brady and the Patriots went 8–4 against Peyton Manning and the Colts.

Brady left the Patriots after the 2019 season. New England's dynasty was over.

In 2021, rookie quarterback Mac Jones led the Patriots to the playoffs. But then New England missed the playoffs two years in a row. After the 2023 season, the team parted ways with Bill Belichick. And Jones was traded away.

Fans pinned their hopes on Rhamondre Stevenson. The running back gained more than 3,000 total yards in his first three seasons.

Mac Jones threw for 3,801 yards and 22 touchdowns as a rookie.

# TOM BRADY

Few people expected big things from Tom Brady when he entered the NFL. The Patriots didn't pick him until the sixth round of the 2000 draft. But he went on to become the greatest quarterback in NFL history. Brady didn't have the strongest arm. However, he was an incredible leader. He was very smart. And he simply refused to lose.

Brady spent 20 seasons with the Patriots. He helped the team win six Super Bowl titles. He also won three Most Valuable Player (MVP) Awards.

**TOM BRADY THREW 541 TOUCHDOWN PASSES DURING HIS 20 YEARS WITH NEW ENGLAND.**

# CHAPTER 5

# MODERN STARS

The Patriots drafted wide receiver Troy Brown in 1993. He spent his whole career with the team. Wes Welker was another sure-handed target. Welker led the NFL in catches three times.

Wes Welker made five straight Pro Bowls from 2008 to 2012.

Strong defenses helped the Patriots build their dynasty. Safety Rodney Harrison was one of the league's hardest hitters. In nine playoff games with the Patriots, he had seven interceptions. Tedy Bruschi was a high-energy linebacker and a great leader.

## CLUTCH KICKER

Adam Vinatieri was one of the greatest kickers in NFL history. He joined the Patriots in 1996. He quickly earned a reputation for making clutch kicks. Vinatieri made the game-winning field goal in two Super Bowls.

Tedy Bruschi spent his entire 13-year career with the Patriots.

Julian Edelman topped 1,000 receiving yards in three different seasons.

Julian Edelman was Brady's favorite target in the late 2010s. Edelman was small by NFL standards. But he was tough. He also knew how to get open. Edelman caught 36 touchdown passes over 11 seasons.

## ON THE FRONT LINE

Guard Logan Mankins was a leader on the offensive line. His size and strength helped create space for running backs. And his pass blocking made Tom Brady's job much easier.

Matthew Judon led New England's defense in the early 2020s. The linebacker recorded 60 tackles in 2021. He matched that number the next season. Judon became known as a strong pass rusher. He racked up 32 sacks in his first three seasons with the Patriots.

Matthew Judon made the Pro Bowl in both of his first two seasons with the Patriots.

# ROB GRONKOWSKI

Rob Gronkowski was one of a kind. New England drafted the tight end in 2010. Fans loved his fun personality. They loved his big-play abilities even more.

Gronkowski quickly became one of Brady's top targets. As a rookie, Gronkowski scored 10 touchdowns. A year later, he had 17 receiving touchdowns. That led the NFL.

**ROB GRONKOWSKI WAS KNOWN FOR SPIKING THE BALL AFTER SCORING.**

Gronkowski spent nine seasons with the Patriots. In that time, he scored 79 receiving touchdowns. That's a team record.

# CHAPTER 6

# TEAM TRIVIA

From 1961 to 1992, the team's logo was known as Pat Patriot. Pat was dressed as a Revolutionary War soldier. But in 1993, the team changed its logo. Some fans call it the "Flying Elvis." That's because it looks a bit like singer Elvis Presley.

New England still uses the Pat Patriot logo on the team's throwback uniforms.

Members of the End Zone Militia fire their guns after a Patriots touchdown.

The End Zone Militia is a big part of Patriots home games. Members of the militia dress up as soldiers. They help fans get excited. They also fire their old-fashioned guns every time New England scores a touchdown.

## FIRST CLASS

In 2017, the Patriots became the first NFL team to buy an airplane. Players and coaches fly across the country in the plane. It's painted red, white, and blue. The Patriots logo and team name appear on each side.

The Patriots' current stadium opened in 2002. The stadium's lighthouse is one of its biggest features. Fans can go to the top of the 22-story structure. A deck gives them a view of nearby Foxborough.

## LIGHTHOUSE TRADITION

Lighthouses are a part of New England culture. They stand along shores to warn sailors when they are close to land. The state of Massachusetts has about 50 lighthouses.

Fans can visit the stadium's lighthouse at any time during the year.

Tom Brady lifts the Super Bowl trophy after beating the Falcons.

The Patriots won six Super Bowl titles during their dynasty. They tied the Pittsburgh Steelers for most in NFL history. But that's not the team's only record. New England has also lost five Super Bowls. The Denver Broncos are the only other team to have lost that many.

## THE COMEBACK

In the 2016 season, the Patriots trailed the Atlanta Falcons 28–3 in the Super Bowl. Just 17 minutes remained. But the Patriots stormed back to tie the game. Then they won in overtime. It was the biggest comeback in Super Bowl history.

# TEAM RECORDS

**All-Time Passing Yards:** 74,571
Tom Brady (2000–19)

**All-Time Touchdown Passes:** 541
Tom Brady (2000–19)

**All-Time Rushing Yards:** 5,453
Sam Cunningham (1973–82)

**All-Time Receiving Yards:** 10,352
Stanley Morgan (1977–89)

**All-Time Receiving Touchdowns:** 79
Rob Gronkowski (2010–18)

**All-Time Interceptions:** 36
Raymond Clayborn (1977–89),
Ty Law (1995–2004)

**All-Time Sacks:** 100
Andre Tippett (1982–93)

**All-Time Scoring:** 1,776
Stephen Gostkowski (2006–19)

**All-Time Coaching Wins:** 266
Bill Belichick (2000–23)

**Super Bowl Titles:** 6
(2001, 2003, 2004, 2014, 2016, 2018)

*All statistics are accurate through 2023.*

# TIMELINE

**1960**

**1970**

**1971**

**1985**

**1996**

The Boston Patriots begin play in the newly formed AFL.

The team changes its name to the New England Patriots.

Quarterback Drew Bledsoe leads the Patriots to the Super Bowl. They lose to the Green Bay Packers.

The AFL and NFL join together. The Patriots become part of the AFC East Division.

The Patriots reach their first Super Bowl. They lose to the Chicago Bears.

**2001**

**2007**

**2016**

**2018**

**2021**

The Patriots have a perfect 16–0 regular season. But they lose to the Giants in the Super Bowl.

Tom Brady leads New England to its sixth Super Bowl title.

Tom Brady replaces the injured Drew Bledsoe. At the end of the season, the team wins its first Super Bowl title.

The Patriots come back from a 28–3 deficit to beat the Falcons in the Super Bowl.

Rookie quarterback Mac Jones leads the Patriots to the playoffs.

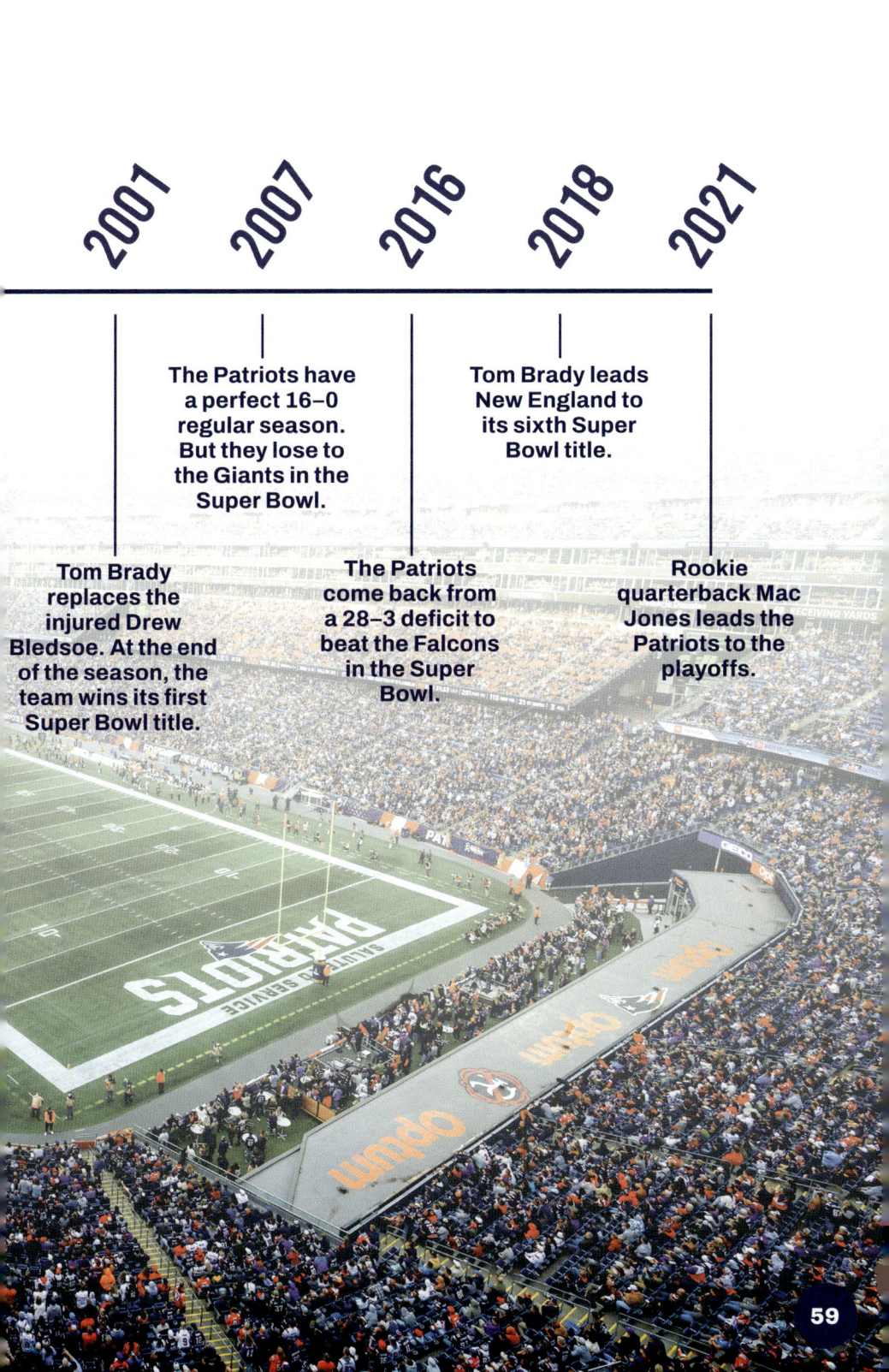

# COMPREHENSION QUESTIONS

*Write your answers on a separate piece of paper.*

1. Write a paragraph that explains the main ideas of Chapter 2.

2. Who do you think was the greatest player in Patriots history? Why?

3. Who did the Patriots beat to win their first Super Bowl title?
   - **A.** Chicago Bears
   - **B.** Green Bay Packers
   - **C.** St. Louis Rams

4. Why did Tom Brady and Peyton Manning have a strong rivalry?
   - **A.** because they grew up in the same city and didn't like each other
   - **B.** because they were two of the best quarterbacks in the NFL
   - **C.** because the Patriots usually won when they played each other

**5.** What does **thrived** mean in this book?

*But he **thrived** with the Patriots. Buoniconti had quickness and good hands. Those skills helped him collect 24 interceptions for New England.*

- **A.** ran very far
- **B.** jumped very high
- **C.** played very well

**6.** What does **reputation** mean in this book?

*He quickly earned a **reputation** for making clutch kicks. Vinatieri made the game-winning field goal in two Super Bowls.*

- **A.** the last two minutes of a title game
- **B.** the things a person is known for
- **C.** the ability to kick the ball very far

*Answer key on page 64.*

# GLOSSARY

**accuracy**
The ability to throw the ball into the proper place and complete passes to receivers.

**clutch**
Having to do with a difficult situation when the outcome of the game is in question.

**division**
In the NFL, a group of teams that make up part of a conference.

**draft**
A system that lets teams select new players coming into the league.

**dynasty**
A team that has a long period of success. The team usually wins several championships.

**interceptions**
Passes that are caught by a defensive player.

**playoffs**
A set of games played after the regular season to decide which team is the champion.

**rivalry**
An ongoing competition that brings out strong emotion from fans and players.

**rookie**
An athlete in his or her first year as a professional player.

**sack**
A play that happens when a defender tackles the quarterback before he can throw the ball.

# TO LEARN MORE

## BOOKS

Coleman, Ted. *New England Patriots All-Time Greats*. Mendota Heights, MN: Press Box Books, 2022.

Holleran, Leslie. *Tom Brady: Gridiron G.O.A.T.* Minneapolis: Lerner Publications, 2024.

Klepeis, Alicia Z. *The New England Patriots.* Minneapolis: Bellwether Media, 2024.

## ONLINE RESOURCES

Visit **www.apexeditions.com** to find links and resources related to this title.

## ABOUT THE AUTHOR

Matt Scheff is an author and artist living in Alaska. He enjoys mountain climbing, fishing, and curling up with his two Siberian huskies to watch sports.

# INDEX

**ANSWER KEY:**
1. Answers will vary; 2. Answers will vary; 3. C; 4. B; 5. C; 6. B